Famous Founding F...

Junior Varsity Squad

S. Adams

Hancock

Morris

Henry

Marshall

Rush

Paine

The Founding Fathers!

Those Horse-Ridin', Fiddle-Playin', Book-Readin', Gun-Totin' Gentlemen Who Started America

By Jonah Winter ☆ Illustrated by Barry Blitt

ATHENEUM BOOKS FOR YOUNG READERS
New York   London   Toronto   Sydney   New Delhi

preamble to The Founding Fathers!

AMERICANS always talk about "the Founding Fathers" as if they were a group of dads who, after a brief huddle, just hauled off and founded America. And Americans are always arguing about them. *They were religious!* says one person. *They **weren't** that religious!* says another. *They were good guys!* says someone else. *They were bad guys!* says another. If the Founding Fathers could hear us now, what would they think? Maybe they'd shake their heads at how badly we misunderstand them. Maybe they'd think it was hilarious that we'd grouped them all together under one name, "the Founding Fathers." It sounds like a rock band! Or a baseball team! George Washington at first, Thomas Jefferson on the mound, Ben Franklin as skipper—what a lineup!

In truth, the men we now call the Founding Fathers were a bunch of guys with stomach issues and wooden legs and problematic personalities—who sometimes couldn't even stand to be in the same room with each other. In truth, these men were not saints. They were imperfect. Sometimes they made no sense. Most claimed to be opposed to slavery, and yet many of those owned slaves. They claimed in their Declaration of Independence that "all men are created equal." And yet, in their Constitution, they made no such claim. The

IT SOUNDS LIKE A ROCK BAND!

Constitution was the original rule book for how the game called "America" would be played. And this Constitution, as they wrote it, made no mention of slavery or voting rights. They left these important issues up to each state to decide for itself. And at that time, in a majority of the states, mostly only white men with money were allowed to vote. In a majority of the states, slavery was perfectly legal. So much for all people being "equal." In creating a bold, new country, the Founding Fathers had also created a lot of problems for future generations to solve.

THEY COULDN'T EVEN STAND TO BE IN THE SAME ROOM AS EACH OTHER!

But, and this is a big "but," the men we now call the Founding Fathers were some of the most **tremendously** smart people who ever lived— just the sort of people you might want to invent a new country (from scratch, without an instruction manual). And like many tremendously smart people, they were often arrogant and stubborn. They argued—**constantly**. Some of them wanted a constitution— others were against it. Some of them wanted one big central government to govern all the states. Others wanted the states to govern themselves. Some of them thought France was a really cool country. And some of them hated France. And some of them just wanted to eat their dinners in peace, without thinking about France at all!

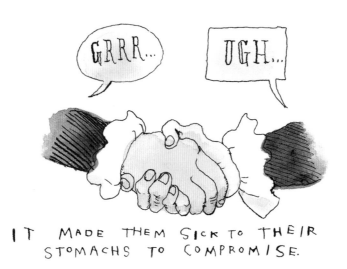

IT MADE THEM SICK TO THEIR STOMACHS TO COMPROMISE.

Basically, the Founding Fathers' opinions were all over the map. They were not like most of America's modern-day politicians who fall into either the Democrat or Republican camp on every single issue. When George

THE FOUNDING FATHERS' OPINIONS WERE ALL OVER THE MAP.

Washington was elected as America's first president in 1789, **there were no political parties**. It was a different country back then, with different problems, and the Fathers tended to think for themselves. The United States that these Fathers founded was not terribly "united"—and definitely not perfect. It was an imperfect nation that reflected all the arguments they'd had in creating it—*and* the **compromises** they had made. Luckily, for Americans, it was also a nation where imperfections could be fixed—even if it took "four score and seven years" or more to fix them. What these Fathers founded was a work in progress—and the model for most modern governments. What they founded was a **foundation** on which to build America—which would later become the most powerful country in the world. It must have been a pretty solid foundation! Here are some of the men who built it.

WHAT THESE FATHERS FOUNDED WAS A WORK IN PROGRESS.

GEORGE WASHINGTON ❧ Father of His Country

(February 22, 1732–December 14, 1799)

GEORGE WASHINGTON

was the first president of the United States of America. Before that, he led the Continental Army in the American Revolution against Great Britain. He was a big guy—and a great dancer. He had no patience for bad manners or loud arguing. As a general, he was fearless, striding through the battlefield while bullets flew past. As president, though, he was extremely cautious, knowing that everything he did would provide an example for all presidents to come. However, one of these examples has never been repeated: Washington is the **only** American president, who, as commander in chief, actually led his army in the field. The enemy? American citizens—working-class Pennsylvanians who had been singled out to pay taxes on the whiskey they were making, even as wealthier merchants were not being taxed. Refusing to pay what they thought were unfair taxes, they staged what is called the Whiskey Rebellion. Washington felt quite strongly that these citizens should quiet down and pay their taxes. And they did. You did not mess with George Washington.

Famous Quotes:

"The fate of unborn millions will now depend, under God, on the courage and conduct of this army."
"My first wish is to see this plague of mankind [war] banished from the earth."
"We ought not to look back unless it is to derive useful lessons from past errors."
"To bigotry no sanction, to persecution no assistance . . ."

HEIGHT: 6' 2"

WEIGHT: 175–200 pounds

SHOE SIZE: 13

POLITICAL LEANING:
 straight (did not lean)

JOBS HELD:
• land surveyor
• British military officer
• commander in chief of Continental Army
• first US president (1789-97)
• gentleman farmer

YEARS SERVED IN BRITISH ARMY: 7

YEARS SERVED IN CONTINENTAL ARMY: 9

YEARS SERVED IN US ARMY: 2

EDUCATION: homeschooled

LANGUAGES MASTERED: English

STANCE ON FRANCE: neutral

HOBBIES: riding horses, fishing

WEALTH: extremely wealthy; $525 million (adjusted for inflation); wealthiest of all presidents

NICKNAME: Father of His Country

POLITICAL PARTY: none

MAIN RESIDENCE: Mt. Vernon, Virginia

LAND OWNED: 58,000 acres

SHEEP OWNED: 600–1000

MULES OWNED: 57

HUMAN SLAVES OWNED: 316

POSITION ON SLAVERY: against it

RELIGIOUS FAITH(S): Anglican/Episcopalian—and supporter of religious freedom and tolerance

ACHIEVEMENTS: started America

OPINION ON BOSTON TEA PARTY: against it

BENJAMIN FRANKLIN ☆ Renaissance Man

(January 17, 1706–April 17, 1790)

BENJAMIN FRANKLIN

was a genius, and perhaps the most endlessly curious American of all time. He was what you call a "Renaissance Man," which means he knew a lot about a lot of different things and was insanely talented. Though he dropped out of school in the fifth grade, Franklin spoke six languages, was an inventor, a scientist, an author, a philosopher, a politician, a publisher, and one of the few Fathers who helped write the Declaration of Independence. He was the oldest of the bunch, and probably the cleverest. He started out life without much money—and ended up one of the hundred richest people in American history. But nothing was more important to him than public service. From being a diplomat, to serving in the Continental and Constitutional Congresses, to serving in the British military, to fighting slavery, to starting America's first public library and first volunteer fire department, Franklin put his money where his mouth was. Maybe that's why his face is on the one-hundred-dollar bill! Plus, many of the things we now call "old sayings" are actually quotes from Benjamin Franklin.

Famous Quotes:

"There was never a good war, or a bad peace."
"Love your enemies, for they tell you your faults."
"In this world nothing can be said to be certain, except death and taxes."
"Remember that time is money."

HEIGHT: 5' 9"

WEIGHT: 220 pounds

POLITICAL LEANING: American

JOBS HELD:
- printer
- author
- publisher
- US ambassador to France
- first US postmaster general
- British colonial military commander
- governor of Pennsylvania

YEARS SERVED IN BRITISH ARMY: 1

EDUCATION: self-educated

LANGUAGES MASTERED: English, French, Latin, Italian, German, and Spanish

STANCE ON FRANCE: loved it!!!

HOBBIES: played harp, violin, and chess

WEALTH: $166 million

NICKNAME: the First American

POLITICAL PARTY: Colonial Quaker Party member, Independent later on

MAIN RESIDENCE: Philadelphia, Pennsylvania

OTHER RESIDENCES: Paris, France, and London, England

LAND OWNED: thousands of acres

HUMAN SLAVES OWNED: 2 (whom he freed)

POSITION ON SLAVERY: absolutely opposed it

RELIGIOUS VIEWS:
- very pro-religion
- tried in vain to start public prayer in Congress
- Christian Deist (he believed in God and the teachings of Jesus, but not in Christ's divinity)

ACHIEVEMENTS:
- invented lightning rod
- invented bifocal glasses
- discovered Gulf Stream current
- wrote funny books

OPINION ON BOSTON TEA PARTY: against it

THOMAS JEFFERSON ☆ America's Coolest Dreamer

(April 13, 1743–July 4, 1826)

THOMAS JEFFERSON

was sort of a mixed bag. Dude wrote that "all men are created equal." But then he also wrote that blacks were inferior humans! Dude said he was totally opposed to slavery. But he owned more than two hundred slaves! Dude thought of himself as a "man of the people"—a regular guy, a farmer, a dude. That's why, as president, he kept sheep on the White House front lawn and wore a bathrobe when greeting foreign leaders. But he was a total rich guy who owned an awesome mansion called Monticello, which he himself designed. That's right, this Founding Dude was also an architect, a scientist, an inventor, a farmer, and an unbelievable reader of books. And check this out: Dude rewrote the Holy Bible, taking out all the stuff he didn't like—such as Christ's divinity! Like Ben Franklin, Jefferson was off-the-charts brilliant—and America's coolest dreamer. And his coolest dream can be found in the totally radical words he wrote in the Declaration of Independence: "We hold these truths to be self-evident: that all men are created equal; that they are endowed by their creator with certain unalienable rights; that among these are life, liberty, and the pursuit of happiness." This was like a TOTALLY new concept that changed the world! (Cool!)

Famous Quotes:

"I abhor war and view it as the greatest scourge of mankind."
"Our liberty depends on the freedom of the press, and that cannot be limited without being lost."
"I cannot live without books."
"It does me no injury for my neighbor to say there are twenty gods or no god."

HEIGHT: 6' 2½"

WEIGHT: thin

SHOE SIZE: 12½

POLITICAL LEANING: forward

JOBS HELD:
- delegate to Second Continental Congress
- governor of Virginia
- US ambassador to France
- first US secretary of state (1789–1793)
- second US vice president (1797–1801)
- third US president (1801–1809)

YEARS SERVED IN THE ARMY: 0

EDUCATION: William & Mary College

LANGUAGES MASTERED: English, Latin, Greek, French, Italian, and Spanish

STANCE ON FRANCE: loved it!

HOBBIES: architect, gentleman farmer, reader/owner of more than 8,000 books, gourmet cook, scientist/inventor, violinist

WEALTH: $212 million (at one point)

NICKNAME: Man of the People

POLITICAL PARTY: Democratic-Republican Party

MAIN RESIDENCE: Charlottesville, Virginia

LAND OWNED: 9,600 acres

CHEESE OWNED: 1,234 pounds

SHEEP OWNED: 93

HOGS OWNED: 123

HUMAN SLAVES OWNED: around 200

POSITION(S) ON SLAVERY: spoke out against it, but was also for it

RELIGIOUS FAITH(S): Christian Deist

ACHIEVEMENTS:
- wrote most of Declaration of Independence
- outlawed slave trade from Africa
- cofounded America's second political party
- purchased Louisiana Territory from France, doubling size of the United States
- hired Lewis and Clark to explore the western territories of North America
- drafted America's first religious freedom law (Virginia Statute for Religious Freedom)

OPINION ON BOSTON TEA PARTY: two thumbs up!

ALEXANDER HAMILTON *The Little Lion*

(January 11, 1755–July 12, 1804)

ALEXANDER HAMILTON

Jefferson may've been one smart green bean, but that old Hamilton was pretty smart too—and them two boys had some different ideas for what'd make America great. Jefferson thought America should be a nation of farmers, governing their own selves. Hamilton thought America should be a nation of big cities and factories and businesses and banks and taxes. Well, in that shoot-out, old Hamilton won! He won most of his shoot-outs. You see, that old Ham was a **fighter**. He'd grown up in the Caribbean, a poor orphan. But I tell you what—he didn't let that stop him. He hightailed it to America and signed right up to fight in the Revolution. And when the war was over, he kept on fightin'. He fought to convince the other Founding Fathers that the CONSTITUTION was a GOOD IDEA. (Some folks didn't want a constitution.) And after that, he hauled off and created a BIG GOVERNMENT BANK for the WHOLE COUNTRY. He liked banks. He liked bankers. He liked rich city folk—'cause that's what he'd become. Well, pardners, the modern-day **America**—controlled by big government, big banks, and corporations—is the country Alexander Hamilton worked hard to shape . . . before he died in an **actual** shoot-out.

Famous Quotes:

"A national debt, if not excessive, will be to us a national blessing."
"Those who do not industrialize become hewers of wood and haulers of water."
"[Thomas Jefferson] is a contemptible hypocrite."

HEIGHT: 5' 7"

POLITICAL LEANING: financial

JOBS HELD:
• lawyer
• Constitutional Convention delegate
• soldier/officer in Continental Army and US Army
• political philosopher/writer
• first US treasury secretary

YEARS SERVED IN MILITIA: 1

YEARS SERVED IN CONTINENTAL ARMY: 6

YEARS SERVED IN US ARMY: 2

EDUCATION: attended King's College (now Columbia University)

LANGUAGES MASTERED: English and French

STANCE ON FRANCE: not a fan

HOBBIES: hunting, fishing, reading, writing, and math

WEALTH: made a lot of money; spent even more money; died in debt

NICKNAME: the Little Lion

POLITICAL PARTY: Federalist (the first American political party, which he launched)

MAIN RESIDENCE: New York, New York

LAND OWNED: 32 acres

SHEEP OWNED: 0

ZEBRAS OWNED: 0

HUMAN SLAVES OWNED: 0

POSITION ON SLAVERY: OPPOSED

RELIGIOUS FAITH(S): Presbyterian; agnostic; and Episcopalian

ACHIEVEMENTS:
• founded Federal Reserve Bank
• wrote more than half of *The Federalist Papers* (it explains the Constitution)
• founded Bank of New York
• founded *New York Post*
• rebuilt Columbia University
• founded US Coast Guard (or "Cutters")
• created first US taxes and tariffs
• more than any other man besides Madison, designed the government of the US

OPINION ON BOSTON TEA PARTY: a big fan!

JOHN ADAMS ❦ His Rotundity

(October 30, 1735–July 4, 1826)

JOHN ADAMS

"sighed, sobbed, and groaned, and sometimes screeched and screamed . . . and sometimes swore." And that's how John Adams described HIMSELF! (Others weren't so kind.) The great unsung hero of the Founding Fathers, "His Rotundity" made a lot of enemies. He spoke bluntly—and often. He had a bad temper. He hated politics and politicians. He was often sad. He had huge doubts that America would even last as a country! He confused people: As a lawyer in colonial Boston, he defended British soldiers accused of murdering American colonists. Some colonists questioned his patriotism. But the way Adams saw it, every citizen deserved a fair trial. He often took unpopular stands. As a member of the Continental Congress, he became one of the first Founding Fathers to call for American independence—originally an unpopular cause! As president, he continued taking on unpopular causes, such as keeping America out of a war with France (many Americans were itching for a war). Then he went and passed the Alien and Sedition Acts, which made it a crime to speak out against him or the American government. In a country where freedom of speech was always a precious right, this did not go over well. John Adams became the first president to lose a re-election.

Famous Quotes:

"Great is the guilt of an unnecessary war."
"In politics, the middle way is none at all."
"Facts are stubborn things; and whatever may be our wishes, our inclinations, or the dictates of our passions, they cannot alter the state of facts and evidence."

HEIGHT: 5' 7"

WEIGHT: not skinny

POLITICAL LEANING: cranky

JOBS HELD:
• lawyer
• delegate to Continental Congresses
• US ambassador to Holland
• US ambassador to Great Britain
• First US vice president
• Second US president

YEARS SERVED IN MILITARY: 0

EDUCATION: Harvard University

LANGUAGES MASTERED: English, Latin, Greek, Hebrew, and French

STANCE ON FRANCE: not a fan

HOBBIES: gardenin', readin', letter-writin', political philosophizin'

WEALTH: $70 million

NICKNAME: His Rotundity

POLITICAL PARTY: Federalist

MAIN RESIDENCE: Quincy, Massachusetts

LAND OWNED: 40 acres

DOGS OWNED: 2

HUMAN SLAVES OWNED: 0

POSITION ON SLAVERY: opposed

RELIGIOUS FAITH(S): devout Unitarian

ACHIEVEMENTS:
• main author of Massachusetts Constitution (oldest written constitution still in use)
• nominated George Washington as commander in chief of Continental Army
• loudest promoter of Declaration of Independence
• as president, averted full-blown war with France
• as president, passed An Act for the Relief of Sick and Disabled Seamen (first US healthcare act)

OPINION ON BOSTON TEA PARTY: two thumbs up!

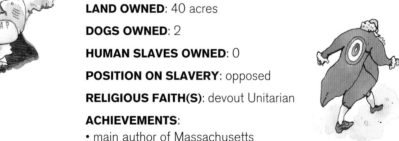

JAMES MADISON — Father of the Constitution

(March 16, 1751–June 28, 1836)

JAMES MADISON

was a tiny man with a tiny voice. He mumbled. He was frail and often sick. And he is often given credit for being THE Founding Father most responsible for designing America's government. You see, this eensy-weensy little man had a PLAN for running America—based on all these books he'd read. Well, boys and girls, Madison's plan got hammered and nailed and kicked around by other Founding Fathers—until it became the US Constitution, America's rule book. Madison's favorite rules had to do with no single branch of government having too much power—and no single majority of people having too much power. Madison feared "democracies," where a majority of uneducated, common people had as much power as a minority of rich people. And so he created a constitution that would protect the "minority" from the "majority." Well, certain Founding Fathers refused to sign off on this PLAN unless it included a list of basic rights for ALL citizens. So, the clever Madison just hauled off and wrote what some folks consider the most important part of the Constitution—the Bill of Rights: freedom of speech, freedom to own guns, and lots of other freedoms that Americans still brag and argue about. Freedom of religion was Madison's favorite. He believed that religion and government should be separate—and he's one reason it is in America. In some ways, James Madison was a giant.

Famous Quotes:

"Religion and government will both exist in greater purity the less they are mixed together."
"A well-instructed people alone can be permanently a free people."
"It is proper to take alarm at the first experiment on our liberties."
"If men were angels, no government would be necessary."

HEIGHT: 5' 4"

WEIGHT: 100 pounds

POLITICAL LEANING: smart

JOBS HELD:
• lawyer
• delegate in Continental Congress
• US representative from Virginia
• fifth secretary of state
• fourth president
• writer/political theorist

YEARS SERVED IN VIRGINIA MILITIA: 7 (non-combat)

EDUCATION: College of New Jersey (now Princeton)

LANGUAGES MASTERED: English, Latin, Ancient Greek, Hebrew, Spanish, and French

STANCE ON FRANCE: *c'est magnifique!*

HOBBIES: reading, horseback riding, chess

WEALTH: $101 million

NICKNAME: Father of the Constitution

POLITICAL PARTY: Democratic-Republican Party (which he cofounded)

MAIN RESIDENCE: Montpelier, Virginia

LAND OWNED: 5,000 acres

HOGS OWNED: 222

PARROTS OWNED: 1

HUMAN SLAVES OWNED: 108

POSITION ON SLAVERY: thought slaves should be freed, then sent to Africa

RELIGIOUS FAITH(S): Deist/Episcopalian

ACHIEVEMENTS:
• wrote plan for US Constitution
• wrote final version of the Bill of Rights
• took notes, recording our most detailed history of Constitution hearings
• co-wrote *The Federalist Papers*
• first president to wear long pants

OPINION ON BOSTON TEA PARTY: not terribly concerned with it

JOHN JAY — The Peacemaker

(December 12, 1745–May 17, 1829)

JOHN JAY

You don't hear as much about him as you do some other Founding Fathers. He was an interesting guy, though—a peacemaker. He was the main guy who got America a peace treaty with Britain at the end of the American Revolution—the Treaty of Paris. Later on, he helped keep America out of another war with Britain through another peace treaty—the Jay Treaty. But many Americans didn't like the Jay Treaty. They thought it was too easy on Britain. And they hated John Jay for this reason. Jay claimed he could find his way across America by the light of his burning effigies. Yikes! Well, he didn't like them much either. What Jay disliked were mobs—big masses of poor people who took to the streets in anger. He did not share Thomas Jefferson's faith in "the people." He thought most people weren't smart enough to govern themselves. Now that doesn't sound very American, does it? But, as an American, Jay had the right to his opinions. For instance, he believed that America should be an officially **Christian nation**—a plan not included in the Constitution. Foiled! BUT he did sometimes get his way. As governor of New York, he freed more slaves than had ever been freed in America. AND, he helped convince the other Founding Fathers to adopt the Constitution. Years later, he had a college named after him in Manhattan.

Famous Quotes:

"Taxes are the price of liberty, the peace and the safety of yourselves and posterity."
"Those who own the country ought to govern it."
"Pure democracy, like pure rum, easily produces intoxication and with it a thousand mad pranks and fooleries."

HEIGHT: 6'

WEIGHT: skinny

POLITICAL LEANING: moderate

JOBS HELD:
• lawyer
• sixth president to Continental Congress
• US ambassador to Spain
• second secretary of state/foreign affairs
• first Supreme Court chief justice
• second governor of New York
• second president of American Bible Society

YEARS SERVED IN MILITARY: 0

EDUCATION: King's College (now Columbia University)

LANGUAGES MASTERED: English, French, Latin, and Greek

STANCE ON FRANCE: not a fan (though he had French blood)

HOBBIES: fighting slavery, reading the Bible

WEALTH: wealthy

POLITICAL PARTY: Federalist

COUNTRIES TRAVELED TO:
• France
• Spain
• Britain

MAIN RESIDENCE: Bedford, New York

LAND OWNED: 750 acres

CATTLE OWNED: a lot

HUMAN SLAVES OWNED: 8

POSITION ON SLAVERY: opposed

RELIGIOUS FAITH(S): extremely devout Episcopalian

ACHIEVEMENTS:
• founded New York Manumission Society (antislavery)
• as New York governor, ended slavery in New York
• negotiated Treaty of Paris
• negotiated Jay Treaty
• wrote *The Federalist Papers* (with Hamilton and Madison)

OPINION ON BOSTON TEA PARTY: thought Tea Partiers deserved fair trials

PATRICK HENRY 🦅 The Actor

(May 29, 1736–June 6, 1799)

PATRICK HENRY

PATRICK HENRY was the greatest actor on the stage of the Founding Fathers. Even though he was very wealthy, he acted like a "man of the people," a good ole boy. And oh how that fiddle-playin' good ole boy could talk. As the most "fiery" public speaker of his time, Henry "fired up" his fellow Founding Fathers with his words. In fact, his words provided some of the first sparks that set the American Revolution aflame, uniting his countrymen in this cause. At the end of his most legendary speech, in which he convinced his fellow Virginians to take up arms against the British army, he supposedly cried out: "Give me liberty . . . *or give me death!*" Then he plunged an invisible dagger into his heart—or so the story goes. If true, those are awfully strong words about "liberty" from a man who owned lots of slaves! After the Revolution, Henry kept on standing up and giving angry speeches—against the Constitution, which he thought would rob individuals and states of their rights. He sliced his opponents to ribbons with his words—and was especially rough on the mumbling Madison. In the end, Henry's forceful speeches helped pressure Madison into adding the Bill of Rights to the Constitution. Sometimes by arguing with someone, you actually help them do the right thing. Arguing is what Americans have always done best.

Famous Quotes:

"I am not a Virginian, but an American."

"If I am asked what is to be done when a people feel themselves intolerably oppressed, my answer is . . . 'overturn the government!'"

"United we stand, divided we fall. Let us not split into factions which must destroy that union upon which our existence hangs."

HEIGHT: 5' 11"

WEIGHT: lean

POLITICAL LEANING: radical

JOBS HELD:
- lawyer
- delegate to the Virginia House of Burgesses
- delegate to Continental Congress
- delegate to Constitution Convention
- first and sixth governor of Virginia

YEARS SERVED IN VIRGINIA MILITIA: 1

EDUCATION: homeschooled and self-educated

LANGUAGES MASTERED/ATTEMPTED: English, Latin, and Greek

STANCE ON FRANCE: not a fan of the French Revolution

HOBBIES: talkin', fiddlin', and hangin' out with folks

WEALTH: wealthy

NICKNAME: Trumpet of the Revolution

POLITICAL PARTY: originally Anti-Federalist (but later Federalist)

MAIN RESIDENCE: Red Hill Plantation, Virginia

OTHER RESIDENCES: Leatherwood Plantation, Virginia

LAND OWNED: 100,000 acres

CATTLE OWNED: more than 167

HUMAN SLAVES OWNED: at one point, 67

POSITION ON SLAVERY: called it "evil," but fought to keep it

RELIGIOUS FAITH(S)/VIEWS: Episcopalian; believed America should be an officially Christian nation

ACHIEVEMENTS:
- wrote/promoted Virginia Stamp Act Resolves (anti-British-taxation laws, which led to the Revolution)
- pressured Madison to write Bill of Rights

OPINION ON BOSTON TEA PARTY: oddly silent (maybe he was busy)

SAMUEL ADAMS · The Angry-Letter-Writer

(September 27, 1722–October 2, 1803)

SAMUEL ADAMS

John Adams claimed that his cousin Samuel was misunderstood and would always be so. Perhaps he was right. The "Sam Adams" most people know is just a myth. *In the myth, Sam Adams was this fiery patriot–a rabble-rouser who could control angry mobs with a wink and a nod. He planned the Boston Tea Party–set it in motion with a "code phrase" at the town hall meeting he was leading–and planned the entire American Revolution!* This myth got started by the British, who had decided Ole Sam was Public Enemy Number One. The true story is more complicated. The real Adams was a first-rate angry-letter-writer and essayist. He was angry about colonists not getting treated as fairly as British citizens–and getting taxed without their say-so. Under pen names, he wrote angry letters in response to his **own** essays! Adams also held many political offices–and did many important things. He was the one who in 1774 proposed that the colonies hold a "Continental Congress"–to figure out how to deal with Britain. What **he** wanted were peaceful protests. He wasn't in favor of the Revolution until it was already happening in late 1775. And there is no proof that he masterminded the Boston Tea Party. He didn't need to fire up Bostonians–they were already fired up. What he **did** do was to **organize** his fellow Colonists to stand up for their rights, **peacefully**–a great American tradition.

Famous Quotes:

"I am no friend to 'Riots, Tumults and unlawful Assemblies.'"

"When people are universally ignorant, and debauched in their manners, they will sink under their own weight without the aid of foreign invaders."

"In monarchy the crime of treason may admit of being pardoned or lightly punished, but the man who dares rebel against the laws of a republic ought to suffer death."

"Mankind are governed more by their feelings than by reason."

HEIGHT: 5' 6"

WEIGHT: solid

POLITICAL LEANING: cautious/radical/moderate/civil-disobedient/patriotic/activist propagandist

JOBS HELD:
• failed maltster (producer of malt)
• failed tax collector
• essay writer
• clerk for the Massachusetts House of Representatives
• delegate to the Continental Congress
• president of the Massachusetts Senate
• governor of Massachusetts

YEARS SERVED IN MILITARY: 0

EDUCATION: Harvard College

LANGUAGES MASTERED: Latin, Greek, and Hebrew

WEALTH: born wealthy; became poor, but died middle class due to an inheritance

NICKNAME: Father of the American Revolution

POLITICAL PARTY: Democratic-Republican Party

MAIN RESIDENCE: Boston, Massachusetts

LAND/PROPERTY OWNED: one medium-size house

DOG OWNED: 1 (a Newfoundland)

HUMAN SLAVES OWNED: 1 (the slave, named Surry, was a "gift" to his wife, and though Adams supposedly offered to free her, she remained a slave)

POSITION ON SLAVERY: absolutely against it

RELIGIOUS FAITH(S): devout Puritan (and anti-Catholic)

ACHIEVEMENTS:
• coined phrase "Boston Massacre"
• wrote "The Rights of the Colonists" (one model for Declaration of Independence)
• initiated Boston Committee of Correspondence
• initiated First Continental Congress
• initiated colonial boycott of British goods

OPINION ON BOSTON TEA PARTY: its biggest fan (but never proven to be the planner)

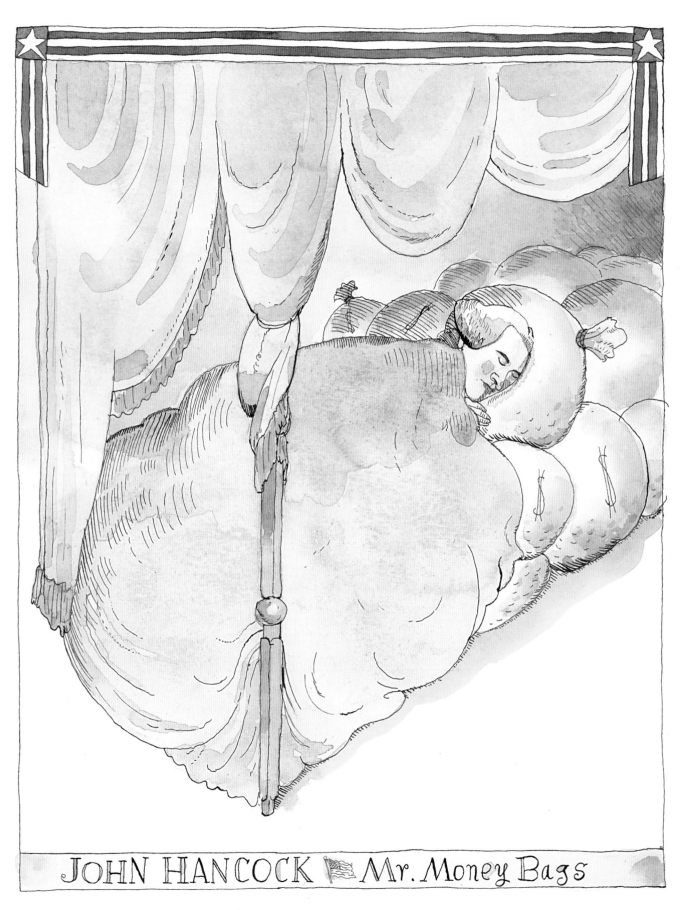

JOHN HANCOCK 🇺🇸 Mr. Money Bags

(January 12, 1737–October 8, 1793)

JOHN HANCOCK

Money money money money money money money money . . . MONEY!!! If you're going to stage a revolution, you better have some cash. Well, boys and girls, John Hancock was Mr. Money Bags—one of the richest men in all the Colonies. And because he was rich, Great Britain taxed him like crazy. That made Hancock mad. But what really turned Mr. Money Bags into a revolutionary was when the British took his boat. That made Hancock mad. It was HIS boat! Mr. Money Bags was accused by Britain of **smuggling** stuff on his boat. This was never proven, though, so the charges were dropped. But, by 1775, Hancock was tied for the Public Enemy Number One spot with Samuel Adams. On April 19, the two of them were fleeing British troops through the woods just before the first shots of the American Revolution were fired. That made Hancock mad, too. So he just hauled off and gave huge amounts of money to the Massachusetts Militia, the "Minutemen." Yep, Hancock definitely put his money where his mouth was—and other places too! As president of the Continental Congress he traveled around in fancy coaches and sparkly clothes—one time escorted by fifty horsemen with drawn sabres! That rubbed a lot of people the wrong way. He looked like a king! Still, the guy had a great signature—the biggest and fanciest (and first) one to be signed to the Declaration of Independence.

Famous Quotes:

"There! His Majesty can now read my name without glasses!" (Legend has it that this is what Hancock exclaimed after signing his name quite largely on the Declaration of Independence. Alas this legend is untrue.)

"I glory in publicly avowing my public enmity to tyranny."

HEIGHT: 5' 11"

WEIGHT: slender

POLITICAL LEANING: ambitious

JOBS HELD:
- shipping merchant
- suspected smuggler
- Boston selectman
- member of the Massachusetts House of Representatives
- first and third governor of Massachusetts
- president of Second Continental Congress
- major general of Massachusetts Militia

YEARS SERVED IN BOSTON CADETS (BRITISH): 3

YEARS SERVED IN MASSACHUSETTS MILITIA: 3

EDUCATION: Harvard College

LANGUAGES MASTERED: Latin, Ancient Greek, and Hebrew

WEALTH: $307 million (at time of death)

POLITICAL PARTY: none

MAIN RESIDENCE: Boston, Massachusetts

LAND OWNED: 22,000 acres

SABRE-WIELDING HORSEMEN RENTED: 50

HUMAN SLAVES OWNED: 6

POSITION ON SLAVERY: opposed and abolished it as governor of Massachusetts

RELIGIOUS FAITH(S): devout Congregationalist

ACHIEVEMENTS:
- first to sign Declaration of Independence
- helped pay for American Revolution

OPINION ON BOSTON TEA PARTY: did not participate, but was a huge fan

THOMAS PAINE The Author

(January 29, 1737–June 8, 1809)

THOMAS PAINE

was a troublemaker who died penniless and friendless. He hated kings, rich people, and pretty much all authority figures. AND some people consider him to be one of the most important Founding Fathers—even though he didn't sign the Declaration of Independence or help frame the Constitution. He was born and bred in England, where he became a pirate and a tax collector. After getting in trouble with the British government, Paine moved to America (with help from Ben Franklin) just before the Revolution. *Revolution?* he must've said to himself. *Sign me up!* The first thing he did in America was to write a book—and not just any book. This book explained, in very simple language, why colonial citizens should want to go to war against Britain. It was a bestseller, and practically every grown-up in America read it. Its title: *Common Sense.* Another thing he wrote, *The American Crisis,* explained why Americans should KEEP fighting the war against Britain. General George Washington even used this book to inspire his tired troops at Valley Forge. There's a common saying that "without the pen of Paine, the sword of Washington would have been wielded in vain." After the Revolution, Paine did things that made his fellow Founding Fathers angry. He joined the French Revolution. He wrote books against religion and slavery. He called for taxes on rich people—and welfare programs for poor people. There was never a more tireless champion of "liberty and justice for all" than Mr. Paine.

Famous Quotes:

"These are the times that try men's souls. The summer soldier and the sunshine patriot will, in this crisis, shrink from the service of their country; but he that stands it now deserves the thanks of man and woman."

"The cause of America is in a great measure the cause of all mankind."

"My country is the world, and my religion is to do good."

"All national institutions of churches, whether Jewish, Christian, or Turkish, appear to me no other than human inventions set up to terrify and enslave mankind, and monopolize power and profit."

HEIGHT: 5' 10"

WEIGHT: athletic

POLITICAL LEANING: 100% revolutionary

JOBS HELD:
- privateer (pirate hired by government)
- servant
- schoolteacher
- tax collector
- tobacco shop owner
- bridge designer
- political philosopher/writer

YEARS SERVED IN CONTINENTAL ARMY: 1

EDUCATION: self-educated

STANCE ON FRANCE: loved the revolutionaries (but hated the aristocrats)

WEALTH: poor

POLITICAL PARTY: none

MAIN RESIDENCE: Bordentown, New Jersey

OTHER RESIDENCES: Paris, London, and many other places

LAND OWNED: 300 acres (a gift from US government)

HUMAN SLAVES OWNED: 0

POSITION ON SLAVERY: against it

RELIGIOUS VIEWS: Deist; against organized religion

ACHIEVEMENTS:
- bestselling author of his time
- wrote stuff that influenced history (*Common Sense*; *The American Crisis*; *Rights of Man*, to name a few)
- took part in American and French Revolutions
- designed what was then the longest iron bridge

OPINION ON BOSTON TEA PARTY: he was in England

GOUVERNEUR MORRIS 🥁 The Aristocrat

(January 31, 1752–November 6, 1816)

GOUVERNEUR MORRIS

James Madison may have come up with the **idea** for the Constitution. But it was a guy named Gouverneur Morris who actually **wrote** it. And no, he was not "governor"—he was . . . ***Gouverneur!*** Anyhow, Gouverneur Morris was an aristocrat. Mob violence sickened him. But Britain's violence also sickened him. So, this aristocrat signed on to the cause for American independence—not an easy decision. He was risking his life AND his family inheritance. (His own mother was a "loyalist" to Britain!) And though he had an arm badly damaged from scalding, Gouverneur joined a revolutionary militia. But where this Gouverneur really shined was at the Constitutional Convention. He spoke more than anybody else—including Madison and Hamilton—in favor of having a constitution. Above all else, he was in favor of reshaping America into **one unified nation**, as opposed to just a **collection of states** (which it was before the Constitution). With this in mind, he wrote what were to become the most famous words in the entire Constitution, "We the people." Patrick Henry preferred "We the states." But Gouverneur prevailed, putting his mark on the whole Constitution by revising, editing, and basically **writing** the final version. Here's what's crazy: Years later he tried to get five northeastern states . . . to secede from America! BUT he failed. AND despite having a wooden leg, Gouverneur Morris was a great dancer (and quite popular with the ladies)!

Famous Quotes:

"We the people of the United States, in Order to form a more perfect Union, establish justice, ensure tranquility, provide for the common defense, promote the general welfare, and secure the blessings of Liberty to ourselves and our Posterity, do ordain and establish this Constitution for the United States of America."

"The mob begins to think and reason. Poor reptiles!"

"There never was, nor never will be a civilized Society without an Aristocracy."

HEIGHT: 6'

WEIGHT: big guy

POLITICAL LEANING: nationalist

JOBS HELD:
- lawyer
- delegate to Continental Congress
- delegate to Constitutional Congress
- US ambassador to France
- US senator

YEARS SERVED IN NEW YORK MILITIA: 1

EDUCATION: King's College (now Columbia University); earned bachelor's degree at age sixteen; earned master's degree at age nineteen

LANGUAGES MASTERED: English, Latin, Ancient Greek, and French

STANCE ON FRANCE: LOVED IT!!!

HOBBIES: dancing, partying, joking around

WEALTH: at least $74 million

POLITICAL PARTY: Federalist

MAIN RESIDENCE: Morrisania Estate (in what is now the South Bronx), New York

OTHER RESIDENCES: London and Paris

LAND OWNED: at least 140,000 acres

HUMAN SLAVES OWNED: 1 (whom he inherited, then freed)

POSITION ON SLAVERY: against it

RELIGIOUS FAITH(S): Episcopalian? Deist? Who knows?!

ACHIEVEMENTS:
- credited with writing most of final draft of US Constitution, most famously the Preamble
- achieved religious tolerance clause in New York Constitution
- cofounder of New York Manumission (antislavery) Society
- played important role in creation of Erie Canal
- helped to create street plan for New York City

OPINION ON BOSTON TEA PARTY: opposed it

BENJAMIN RUSH ★ *Father of American Medicine*

(January 4, 1746–April 19, 1813)

BENJAMIN RUSH

thought that the American Revolution was just the beginning of the REAL revolution. The real revolution involved changing how people thought and acted. Rush was what we call a "social reformer"—a person who wants to make the world a better place. As a member of the First Continental Congress, he had such strong opinions on so many topics that before he knew it, he was voted out of office. His opinions? He thought slavery was EVIL, and he wouldn't stop talking about it. He was opposed to democracy, where the majority rules. And he would argue with anybody. The problem was, he didn't always make sense. Though he was America's most respected doctor, he practiced bloodletting on his patients excessively—even when other doctors knew better. And though he hated slavery and argued that black people were just as smart as white people, he ALSO thought that being black was a kind of skin disease . . . that could be **cured**! He claimed all his inspiration came from Christianity. He wanted American kids to be taught Christianity in public schools. AND he was one of the first Americans to push for free public schools—and education for girls.

Famous Quotes:

"I have alternately been called an aristocrat and a Democrat. I am neither. I am a Christocrat."

"The American war is over, but this is far from being the case with the American Revolution."

"A simple democracy . . . is one of the greatest of evils."

HEIGHT: 5' 9"

WEIGHT: average

POLITICAL LEANING: revolutionary

JOBS HELD:
- doctor
- university professor of medicine/chemistry
- surgeon general of Continental Army
- treasurer of US Mint
- writer

YEARS SERVED IN CONTINENTAL ARMY: 1

EDUCATION: College of New Jersey (Princeton), from which he graduated at age fourteen, and University of Edinburgh Medical School

LANGUAGES MASTERED: French, Spanish, Italian, Latin, and Ancient Greek

HOBBIES: writing essays and letters (two thousand pages' worth!)

WEALTH: upper-middle class

NICKNAMES: Father of American Psychiatry, Father of American Medicine

POLITICAL PARTY: none

MAIN RESIDENCE: Philadelphia, Pennsylvania

OTHER RESIDENCES: Edinburgh, Scotland, and London, England

LAND OWNED: 44 acres (at one point)

HUMAN SLAVES OWNED: 1 (whom he freed after nearly twenty years)

POSITION ON SLAVERY: against it

RELIGIOUS FAITH(S): extremely devout Universalist; Presbyterian; Episcopalian

ACHIEVEMENTS:
- cofounded Pennsylvania Abolitionist Society
- pioneered American Sunday school movement
- founded America's first free hospital for poor people
- cofounded one of America's first girls' schools
- cofounded Pennsylvania Prison (reform) Society
- trained three thousand medical students
- treated one hundred patients a day during 1793 yellow fever epidemic in Philadelphia
- revolutionized treatment of the mentally ill
- proposed a US Department of Peace

OPINION ON BOSTON TEA PARTY: huge fan

JOHN MARSHALL 🔔 The Great Chief Justice

(September 24, 1755–July 6, 1835)

JOHN MARSHALL

was like a frontier marshal—and the Supreme Court was his frontier. Before Marshall, the full meaning and power of the Supreme Court had yet to be discovered. Yes, it was the highest court in the land—and the most important part of the "judicial branch" of America's government. But no one much knew what that meant. Well, pardner, under Marshall's rule as chief justice, the Supreme Court came to have as much power as the president—and Congress. Under Marshall, the federal court system became the branch of government that has the final word on what the Constitution means. It became the final word on what was—and wasn't—"constitutional." This new power didn't sit too well with Marshall's cousin, President Thomas Jefferson. Jefferson thought that judges shouldn't have so much power. Marshall thought that neither Jefferson nor any president had the right to tell the Supreme Court what to do. It was a regular showdown. Jefferson thought the states should mainly govern themselves. But Marshall made sure that state laws did not break the supreme law of the land, the Constitution. And he did this for over thirty years, longer than any other Supreme Court justice. Because his career as a judge started only in 1801, after the "founding" period, he is often left off Founding Fathers lists. But John Marshall brought law and order to the country that he helped to found. HYAH!

Famous Quotes:

"The people made the Constitution, and the people can unmake it. It is the creature of their own will, and lives only by their will."

"It is emphatically the province and duty of the judicial department to say what the law is."

HEIGHT: 6' (more or less)

WEIGHT: slender

POLITICAL LEANING: toward the Constitution

JOBS HELD:
- lawyer
- member of Virginia House of Delegates
- delegate to Constitutional Convention
- member of House of Representatives
- fourth secretary of state
- fourth Supreme Court chief justice

YEARS SERVED IN CONTINENTAL ARMY: 5

EDUCATION: homeschooled; College of William and Mary

LANGUAGES MASTERED: English and Latin

STANCE ON FRANCE: mixed feelings (hated the government, loved the culture)

WEALTH: quite wealthy

NICKNAME: the Great Chief Justice

POLITICAL PARTY: Federalist

MAIN RESIDENCE: Richmond, Virginia

OTHER RESIDENCE: Washington, DC

LAND OWNED: more than 200,000 acres

HUMAN SLAVES OWNED: 10 (at one point)

POSITION ON SLAVERY: thought slaves should be freed, then sent to Africa

RANDOM FACT: The day of Marshall's funeral, the Liberty Bell was rung in his honor; then it suddenly cracked, never to be rung again.

RELIGIOUS FAITH: Episcopalian

ACHIEVEMENTS:
- transformed Supreme Court's power
- presided over more than one thousand Supreme Court decisions
- helped negotiate end to Quasi-War with France (as secretary of state)

OPINION ON BOSTON TEA PARTY: believed it was necessary

First Amendment to the Preamble of The Founding Fathers!

I. WHAT MAKES A FOUNDING FATHER A FOUNDING FATHER?

The term "Founding Fathers" was first used by President Warren G. Harding in 1918. Since then, it has become one of the most popular historical terms in America. Most historians agree that in order to be a Founding Father, you had to have (a) signed the Declaration of Independence, and/or (b) helped to "frame" the US Constitution. There are certain Founding Fathers, however, who did **neither** but are nonetheless regarded as Founding Fathers by many historians—because they helped shape a new nation. This book is a showcase of the most famous Founding Fathers, though it is by no means a complete or perfect list. Our understanding of history is always changing.

WHAT MAKES A FOUNDING FATHER A FOUNDING FATHER?

II. SOME THINGS THEY ARGUED ABOUT

The Declaration of Independence: On July 4, fifty-six of the Founding Fathers agreed on a formal, written Declaration of Independence from Great Britain. This was not an easy decision. Not long before this date, many of the Fathers had still held out hope that the colonies could work out their problems with Britain without declaring independence. By creating this document, these upstanding, respected, wealthy citizens of the British Crown . . . were becoming outlaws! They could be arrested—or hanged! This Declaration would mean WAR. And many of the Founding Fathers had big doubts that America could win such a war. And they argued and argued and argued. BUT on August 2, 1776, they signed this declaration.

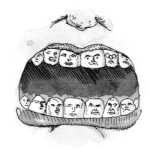

THEY ARGUED AND ARGUED AND ARGUED AND ARGUED...

The United States Constitution: The Constitution is a set of rules. These rules provide the framework for America's government. When it was first proposed in 1787, many of the Fathers were totally opposed to it. They thought it would deprive Americans of their rights and freedoms. They thought it would put power in the hands of only the wealthy and educated, and that this was UNFAIR. What they wanted instead was democracy, where the people govern themselves. They wanted the states to be able to make their own laws and not have to answer to a national constitution. They feared a big "central government" that would have too much power over the states. The pro-constitution Fathers argued that if America were to survive and grow as a country, it would need to be more united. It would need one central

THE UNITED STATES CONSTITUTION

government that controlled all the states. And it would need a constitution that applied to all Americans. The pro-constitution Fathers won, and created the Constitution. But the anti-constitution Fathers forced them to add the Bill of Rights, which helped protect certain basic rights and freedoms of common people. Americans are still adding to the Constitution . . . and arguing about it, constantly. Like America itself, it is a Work in Progress.

Religion: America, especially in New England, had been settled in large part by people who wanted the freedom to practice whatever religion they pleased. In Europe, you see, many governments tried to tell their people how to worship. This was a big issue for the Founding Fathers, who practiced a variety of Christian faiths. So, the Constitution they framed made it clear that America's government should not establish any specific religious faith as the official religion of America. The Constitution made it clear that all Americans have the right to practice their own religious beliefs—or not. HOWEVER, even though this became the law of the land, the Founding Fathers disagreed on this topic. Many thought America should be an officially **Christian** nation—that children should be forced to learn about the Bible in school, that every session of Congress should open with a Christian prayer. And Americans still disagree on the topic to this day.

Strong Central Government vs. States Rights: Some of the Founding Fathers thought that each state in America should get to mainly control itself and make its own laws. Other Founding Fathers thought that was a bad idea—they thought that one central government should control all the states. What they came up with was a compromise. Certain matters—such as who has the right to vote, and laws regarding slavery—would be left up to the states to decide. But there would also be one big central government that controlled the whole country, and one constitution with rules and laws and freedoms that applied to all the states. Even after this compromise, though, the Fathers argued bitterly about states rights versus central government. And more than two hundred years later, Americans are still arguing about it.

STRONG CENTRAL GOV'T VS. STATES' RIGHTS

Slavery: Back in the 1700s, people all over America owned slaves—in the north and the south. And though some people spoke out against slavery, those people were in the minority. Slavery was popular. But it was also an emotional topic that caused a lot of arguing. Most of the Founding Fathers were opposed to slavery . . . in theory. But slaves were a crucial part of the American economy, and many of the Founding Fathers owned slaves— even many of those who claimed to be morally opposed to slavery! Certain southern Fathers (and especially the ones from North Carolina, South Carolina, and Georgia) were more pro-slavery than most of the other Fathers. So, in order to get these particular **southern** Founding Fathers to agree to the new Constitution, the **other** Founding Fathers had to leave out the topic of slavery altogether—and leave it up to the individual states to decide. It wasn't until 1865 that the Constitution was finally amended to outlaw slavery in all the states. Unfortunately, a bloody Civil War between the north and the south happened first.

Democracy: Back in the 1700s, "democracy" meant a system of government by which the people govern themselves—where anyone can vote, where anyone can run for office, and where the majority rules. The America that the Founding Fathers founded was not a pure democracy. It was a "constitutional republic"—a government guided by a constitution; a nation where not just anyone could vote or run for office. Most of the Founding Fathers thought that America should be governed by educated, wealthy people—people smart enough to run a country. These Fathers (including Hamilton, Madison, Jay, Morris, and Rush) were opposed to "majority rule." These Fathers were against the riffraff of America (the "majority") being in control—which they thought of as "mob rule." That would not be good for the "minority" of wealthy people. However, there was also a vocal group of Founding Fathers who were pro-democracy (including Jefferson, Henry, and Paine). Though they didn't win the argument, their pro-democracy views helped shape the country America would later become. For instance, in current-day America, most adult citizens have the right to vote—regardless of color, gender, creed, or wealth. **And voting is the most important expression of democracy.**

Foreign Wars: The Founding Fathers were divided on whether or not it was a good idea to get involved in the wars of other countries. They could not agree on this topic. Nor can current-day Americans.

Taxes: Taxes are monies that the people have to pay to the government—to help pay for stuff like roads and armies and schools and stuff. Before the Revolution, the British government was charging Americans taxes without their consent—and without giving them representatives in Parliament. This made Americans mad. "No taxation without representation!" they cried. And this became the rallying cry for the American Revolution. It wasn't that colonists didn't want to pay taxes. It was that they had no say over what taxes they paid and had no representatives in the British Parliament. As British citizens, they thought this was unfair. In modern-day America, many Americans still complain that the taxes are "unfair." But these complaints are different from the colonists' complaints. Modern-day Americans DO have some say over which taxes they pay—by having the right to elect their own representatives to Congress. The main exception to this is, oddly enough, in Washington, D.C., the nation's capital. Washington has no representatives in Congress: *taxation without representation!*

BOSTON TEA PARTY

Boston Tea Party: On December 16, 1773, a group of colonists boarded three ships containing tea that Britain was forcing the colonies to purchase. Very quietly and peacefully, these men dumped the tea into Boston Harbor. Later on, this became known as the Boston Tea Party. It was one of the events that pushed America on the path toward revolution. Though many Founding Fathers applauded this bold act, not all the Fathers approved of it. Some Founding Fathers took "destruction of private property" very seriously—and were horrified at the actions of the Tea Partiers. Most horrified of all . . . was George Washington.

USEFUL WEBSITES, AS WELL AS DOCUMENTS, BOOKS, AND ARTICLES BY AND ABOUT THE FOUNDING FATHERS

"The Anti-Federalist Papers": constitution.org/afp.htm

Charters of Freedom, "Bill of Rights": archives.gov/exhibits/charters/bill_of_rights_transcript.html

——, "The Constitution of the United States": archives.gov/exhibits/charters/constitution_transcript.html

——, "Declaration of Independence": archives.gov/exhibits/charters/declaration_transcript.html

Gardener, Andrew G., "How Did Washington Make His Millions?": history.org/foundation/journal/winter13/washington.cfm

George Washington's Mount Vernon: mountvernon.org

Hamilton, Alexander, James Madison, and John Jay, *The Federalist Papers*, Jon Roland, ed.: constitution.org/fed/federa00.htm

Knobloch, Muriel, "Gouverneur Morris and His Contributions to the Development of New York": *The Hudson River Valley Regional Review*: hudsonrivervalley.org/review/pdfs/hvrr_16pt1_knobloch.pdf

Library of Congress, "Alien and Sedition Acts: Primary Documents of American History": loc.gov/rr/program/bib/ourdocs/Alien.html#American

——, "The American Founders Online: An Annotated Guide to Their Papers and Publications": compiled by Jurretta Jordan Heckscher: loc.gov/rr/program/bib/founders/#samuel

"The Life and Morals of Jesus of Nazareth": *The Bible*: uuhouston.org/files/The_Jefferson_Bible.pdf

Madison, James, "Memorial and Remonstrance Against Religious Assessments": religiousfreedom.lib.virginia.edu/sacred/madison_m&r_1785.html

——, "Selected Works of James Madison," Jon Roland, ed.: constitution.org/jm/jm.htm

Massachusetts Historical Society: "Thomas Jefferson Papers: Farm Book": masshist.org/thomasjeffersonpapers/farm

——, "Thomas Jefferson Papers: Notes on the State of Virginia Manuscript": masshist.org/thomasjeffersonpapers/notes

National History of Health, "An Act for the Relief of Sick and Disabled Seamen": history.nih.gov/research/downloads/1StatL605.pdf

"The Papers of Benjamin Franklin": franklinpapers.org/franklin

Red Hill—Patrick Henry National Memorial: redhill.org

Rush, Benjamin, "Essays: Literary, Moral & Philosophical": english.byu.edu/facultysyllabi/KLawrence/RUSH.essays.pdf

——, "Observations Intended to Favour a Supposition That the Black Colour (As It Is Called) of the Negroes Is Derived from the Leprosy": *Transactions of the American Philosophical Society*: jstor.org/stable/1005108

Thomas Jefferson's Monticello: monticello.org

Virginia Historical Society, "Thomas Jefferson and the Virginia Statute of Religious Freedom": vahistorical.org/collections-and-resources/virginia-history-explorer/thomas-jefferson

SOME ADDITIONAL PREAMBLES

A Note about "Livestock Owned" Figures Listed for Founding Fathers

Given the fluctuating nature of livestock (regularly dying, being born, or sold), it is difficult to list any one amount that is accurate for the entirety of each Founding Father's period of ownership. Therefore, the figures chosen pertain to one year and one inventory. Hopefully, these figures will give the reader an idea of how many hogs or sheep (or parrots) each Founding Father generally owned at any given point.

A Note about "Human Slaves Owned" Figures Listed for Each Founding Father

The figures here do not reflect the entire period of ownership but just one year and one inventory. Again, these figures are only intended to give the reader an idea of how many slaves each Founding Father generally owned at any given point. Where exact information is not available, the figures listed are averages.

A Note about "Land Owned" Figures Listed for Each Founding Father

Many of the Founding Fathers were regularly buying and selling land parcels. The figures here reflect the amount of land owned at a point for which an exact figure is now available. In some instances, the exact figure is difficult to determine, and so words such as "more than" or "nearly" have been used. Again, these figures will hopefully give the reader a general idea of the scope of each Founding Father's land holdings (which would have been greater or lesser at different points). In any case, the figures will be useful in differentiating between Fathers who owned very little land—and those who owned hundreds of thousands of acres.

A Note about the "Wealth" Figures Listed for Each Founding Father

The figures here (where available) reflect the net worth of each Founding Father at its peak. Net worth includes not just money, but also the monetary value of all land holdings and property (including human property). The dollar amounts listed are estimations based on the Founding Father's net worth as adjusted for inflation to 2014 American dollar value. There are many ways of estimating wealth. The method used here involves measuring the individual's net worth against the entire worth of America. It's kind of complicated.

For Ed Denmead,
the Founding
Father of SMEDJ

–J. W.

To my father

–B. B.

ATHENEUM BOOKS FOR YOUNG READERS
An imprint of Simon & Schuster Children's Publishing Division
1230 Avenue of the Americas, New York, New York 10020

For information about special discounts for bulk purchases, please contact Simon &
Schuster Special Sales at 1-866-506-1949 or business@simonandschuster.com.
The Simon & Schuster Speakers Bureau can bring authors to your live event. For more
information or to book an event, contact the Simon & Schuster Speakers Bureau at
1-866-248-3049 or visit our website at www.simonspeakers.com.
Book design by Debra Sfetsios-Conover
The text for this book is set in Akzidenz Std.
The illustrations for this book are rendered in pen, ink, and watercolor.
Manufactured in China
1014 SCP
First Edition
10 9 8 7 6 5 4 3 2 1
Library of Congress Cataloging-in-Publication Data
Winter, Jonah, 1962-
The Founding Fathers!: Those horse-ridin', fiddle-playin', book-readin', gun-totin'
gentlemen who started America / Jonah Winter; illustrated by Barry Blitt. — 1st ed.
p. cm.
ISBN 978-1-4424-4274-0 (hardcover)
ISBN 978-1-4424-4275-7 (eBook)
1. Founding Fathers of the United States—Juvenile literature. 2. United States—History—
Revolution, 1775–1783—Juvenile literature. I. Blitt, Barry, ill. II. Title.
E302.5.W77 2015
973.3—dc23 2012030311

Acknowledgments

Thanks to Thomas Marshall Twiss, reference librarian for the Pittsburgh Public Library, for his research and assistance in determining wealth figures for the Founding Fathers.

Thanks, too, to Anna Berkes, research librarian for the Jefferson Library (Thomas Jefferson Foundation), for her research and assistance in determining Thomas Jefferson's land holdings.

And thanks, especially, to my editor Caitlyn Dlouhy, for championing and shepherding this project—and staying the course through an editing and revision process that at times seemed to take its cue from the Founding Fathers themselves! (Arguing is always what Americans have done best—or at least writers and editors.)

–J. W.

Fourteen of the Most

Varsity Squad

Washington

DISCARD

Franklin

J. Adams

Madison

Hamilton